Christopher ROUSE

KAROLJU

For Chorus and Orchestra

Choral Score

HENDON MUSIC

BOOSEY & HAWKES

DISTRIBUTED BY
HAL•LEONARD®

Contents

1. Ob vix abdurat (Latin) / Page 1

2. Än kännas i på (Swedish) / Page 6

3. Je son de la feuli que l'aime (French) / Page 14

4. Siempre los mascara (Spanish) / Page 22

5. Procession of the Three Kings (Percussion) / Page 26

6. Ob vix abdurat (reprise) / Page 32

7. Bozhe za kranit vsye (Russian) / Page 35

8. Nemám dobrá se stále znova (Czech) / Page 40

9. O die zimmer dank (German) / Page 49

10. Ob vix abdurat (reprise) / Page 61

11. Spera dolci (Italian) / Page 65

Appendix: Program notes and "perductions" of the texts by the composer

Commissioned by the Baltimore Symphony Orchestra with the generous assistance of Randolph S. Rothschild and the Barlow Endowment for Music Composition at Brigham Young University.

KAROLJU

Choral Reduction

Christopher Rouse

LCB 260

Printed in U.S.A.

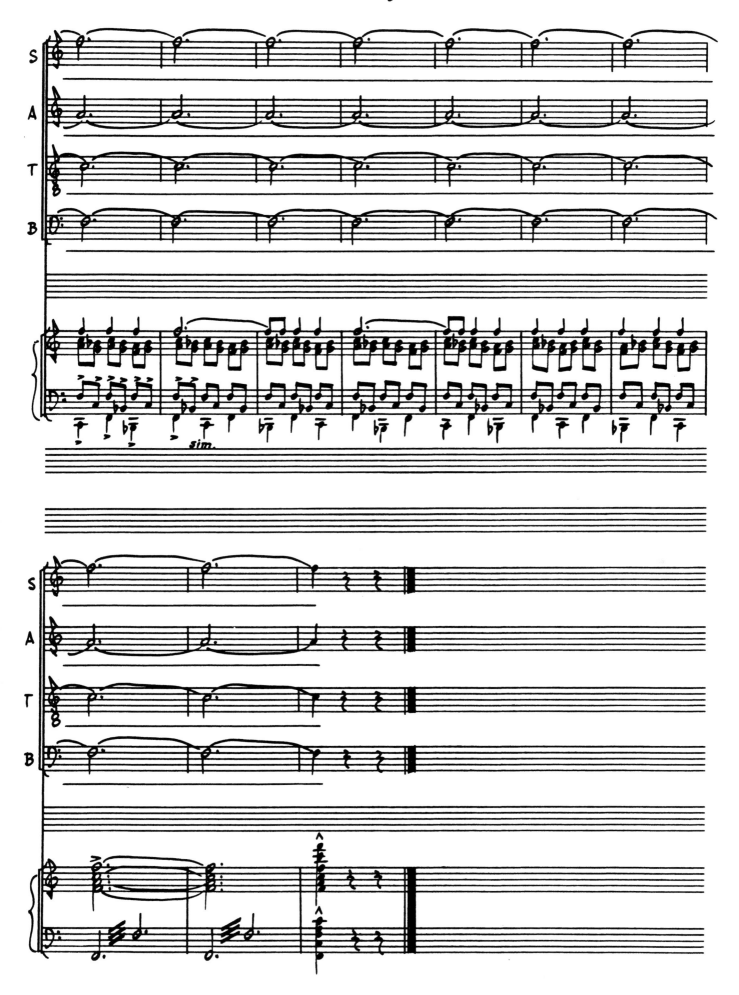

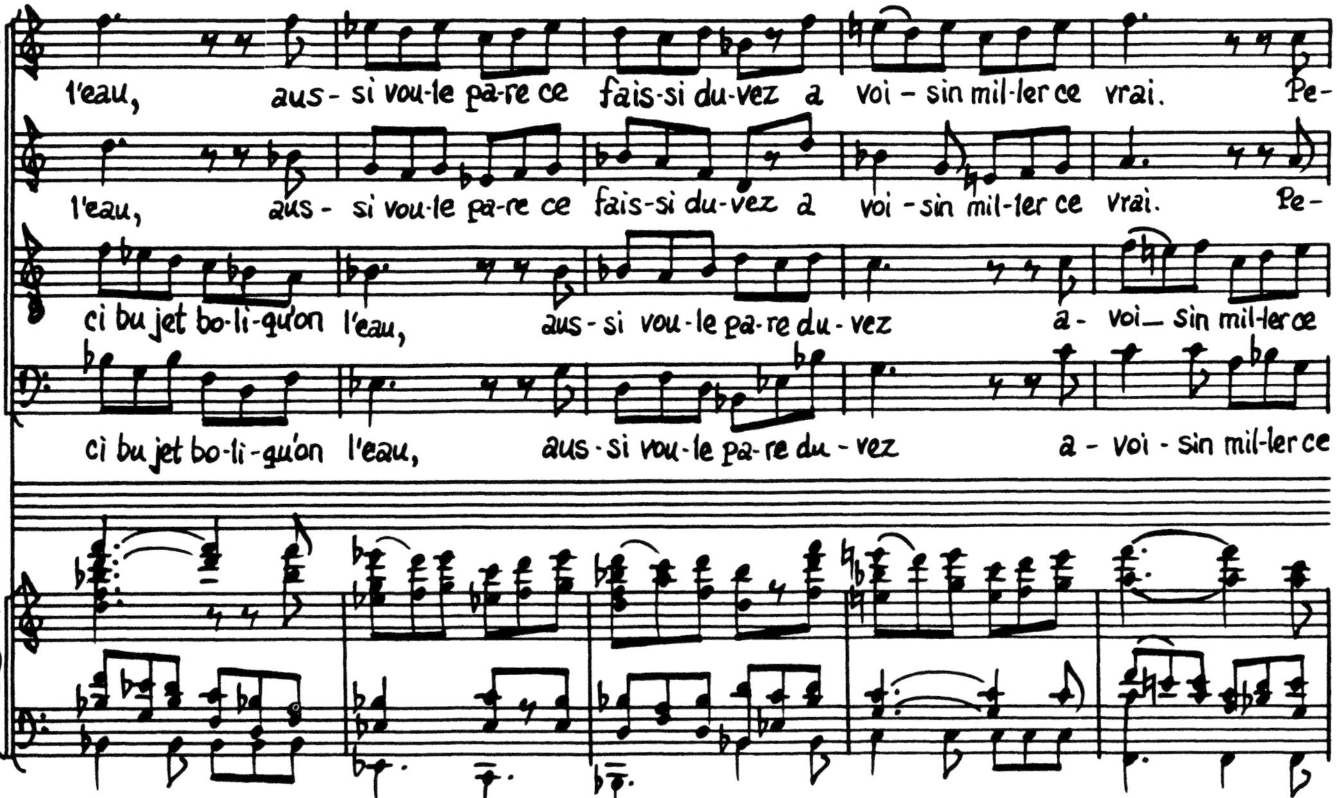

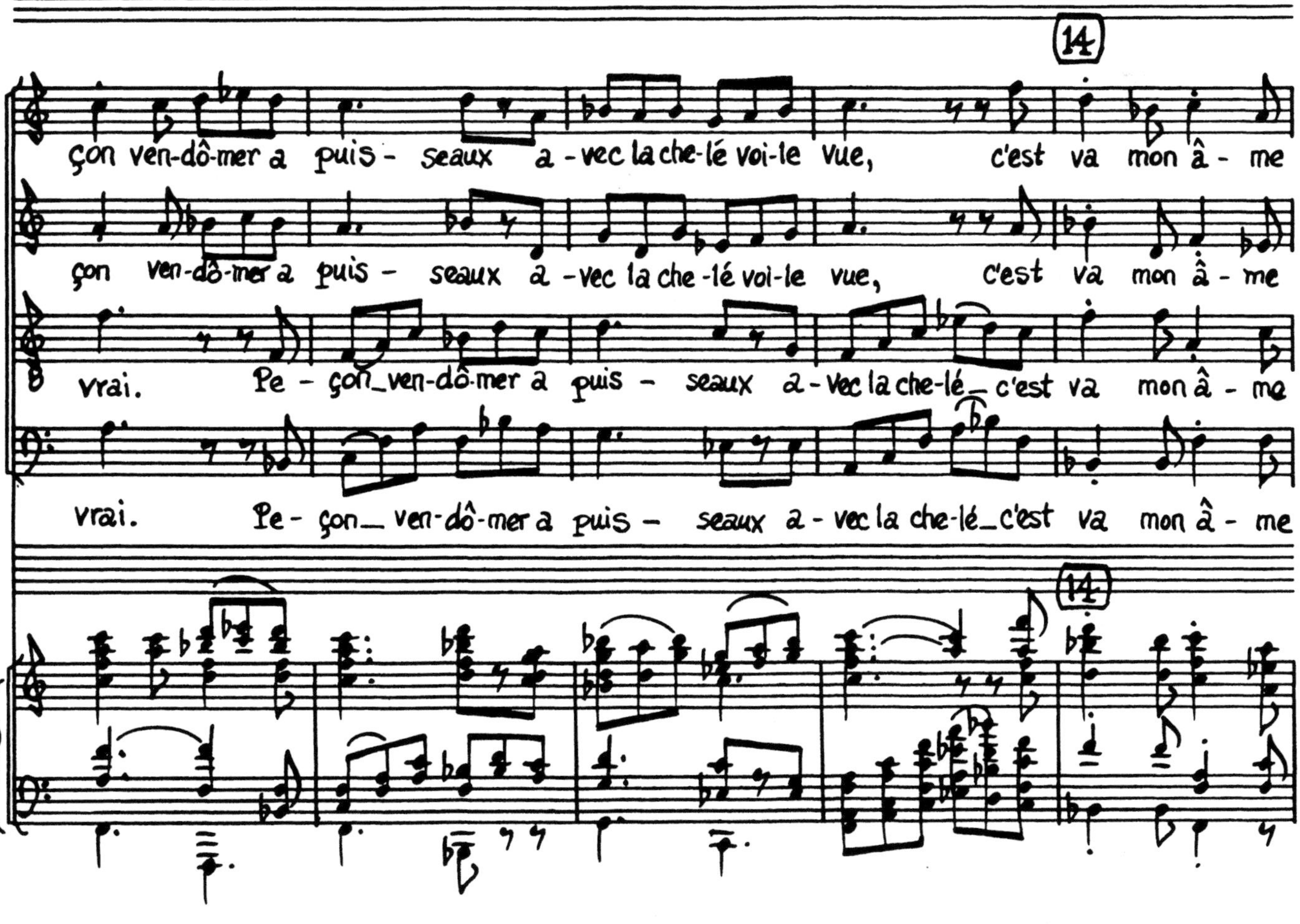

S: es - que se - det ce - le - bra - tur ful - ma!

A: es - que se - det ce - le - bra - tur ful - ma!

T: es - que se - det ce - le - bra - tur ful - ma!

B: es - que se - det ce - le - bra - tur ful - ma!

⑦ RUSSIAN

36

♩=60

T: Bo-zhe za kra-nit vsye do-moi vo-zhmo-lem shto dru-

T: Bo-zhe za kra-nit vsye do-moi vo-zhmo-lem shto dru-

B: Bo-zhe za kra-nit vsye do-moi vo-zhmo-lem shto dru-

B: Bo-zhe za kra-nit vsye do-moi vo-zhmo-lem shto dru-

T
T
B
B
Gos-po-di-ya sto-mu vye-le bo-ro ka-mo- zhe, sla-va, sla-va byet po-gi bel ska-zi vai to-lu-moi
Gos-po-di-ya sto-mu vye-le bo-ro ka-mo -zhe, sla-va, sla-va byet po-gi bel ska-zi vai to-lu-moi
Gos-po-di-ya sto-mu vye-le bo-ro ka-mo-zhe, sla-va, sla-va byet po-gi bel ska-zi vai to-lu-moi
Gos-po-di-ya sto-mu vye-le bo-ro ka-mo-zhe, sla-va, sla-va byet po-gi bel ska-zi vai to-lu-moi
rit. al. . . . . . ♩=104
Tempo I° (♩=60)
39
vuota
mp
p
mf
bat ut-kyo ve-zhe-la - - - - - - yo. Po-shol sam
bat ut-kyo ve-zhe-la - - - - - - yo. Po - shol sam
bat ut-kyo ve-zhe-la - - - - - - yo. Po - shol sam
bat ut-kyo ve-zhe - la - - - - - - yo. Po - shol sam
rit. al. . . . . . ♩=104
Tempo I° (♩=60)
39
vuota
mp
p
mfzp
mp

S zi-či má, šes- tak u-vém e je-maž pos-va hlu-ryl ba-ču ném - vit!

A zi-či má, šes- tak u-vém e je-maž pos-va hlu-ryl ba-ču ném - vit!

T zi-či má, šes-tak u-vém e je-maž pos-va hlu-ryl ba-ču ném - vit!

B zi-či má, šes- tak u-vém e je-maž pos-va hlu-ryl ba-ču ném - vit!

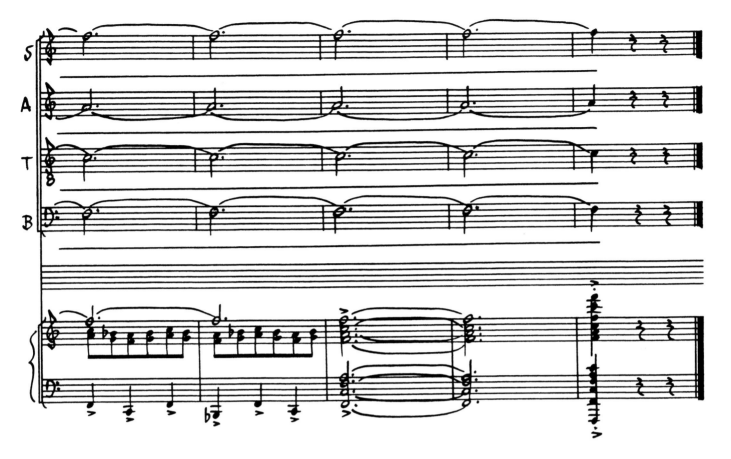

KAROLJU

Program note by the composer

Two paths led to the composition of *Karolju*. The first was the great body of Christmas carols written over the centuries, a collection I value as highly for their meaning as for their glorious music. The second was Carl Orff's *Carmina Burana*, which made an unforgettable impression upon me when I first heard it in March 1963 performed by the Baltimore Symphony Orchestra and the Howard University Choir under the direction of Warner Lawson.

In the early 1980s, I conceived of a plan to compose a collection of Christmas carols couched in an overall form similar to that of *Carmina Burana*, but it was not until 1989, when the work was commissioned by the Baltimore Symphony, that I was able to begin serious thought about it, although I had composed several of the carols in my mind over the preceding years.

As I wished to compose the music first, the problem of texts presented itself. Finding pre-composed texts to fit already existing music would have been virtually impossible. As I did not trust my own ability to devise a poetically satisfying text, I decided to write my own texts in a variety of languages (in order: Latin, Swedish, French, Spanish, Russian, Czech, German, and Italian); although these texts use words and phrases appropriate to the Christmas season, they are not intelligibly translatable for long periods of time. It was rather my intent to match the sound of the language to the style of the carol to which it was applied.

I also elected to compose music that was direct and simple in its tonal orientation, music that would not seem out of place in a medley of traditional Christmas carols. Those who know other of my works may be surprised - some even distressed - by *Karolju*. While I can assert with assurance that this does not represent a 'change of direction' for me and thus constitutes an isolated example, *Karolju*, nonetheless, is a piece that I 'mean' with all my heart, one which I hope will help instill in listeners the special joy of the season it depicts, which I remember so well. As a result, I decided to eschew complexity or over-subtlety of utterance, preferring instead to compose music that was straightforward in its melody, harmony, and orchestration. Except for a paraphrase of the coda to the 'O Fortuna' movements in *Carmina Burana* (which I have used in Nos. 1 and 10 of *Karolju* and which constitute a small homage to Orff) and for a four-measure phrase in No. 3 which I borrowed from *The Nutcracker* (which Tchaikovky himself cribbed from an anonymous 18th-century minuet), all of the music in *Karolju* is my own. In an attempt to provide some unity for the work, certain melodic phrases or chord progresssions have been employed in several of the carols.

Karolju was completed in Fairport, New York on November 13, 1990 and is dedicated to my daughter Alexandra, who celebrated her first Christmas that year. With a duration of approximately 25 minutes, it is scored for large SATB chorus and an orchestra consisting of two flutes (second doubling piccolo), two oboes, two clarinets, two bassoons, four horns, three trumpets, three trombones, tuba, timpani, percussion (four players), harp, and strings.

KAROLJU

"Perductions"

1. Ob vix abdurat

My faith and my strength are renewed this Christmas Day,
    Sent from on high by God above,
Who gives to mankind His only begotten son
    As a sign of His holy love.

    Praise Him! Praise the Lord, my people;
    Praise Him to the skies!
    It is through His grace and His sacred gift
    That our salvation lies.
    Lord God! Lord, we give thanks
    For we shall be redeemed
    By this child born of Mary
    Of whom Elijah dreamed!

2. Än kännas i på

High up in a tree, the Christmas bird sings,
Calling far and wide the Christmas morn,
Trumpeting his song, he spreads his wings,
Proclaims the tidings - "Christ is born!"

    He spreads his wings
    And sings his song,
    Proclaims the tidings
    All day long.
    When the sun sets
    And the deep night falls,
    The Christmas bird
    Still calls, and he calls, and he calls -
    "Kikiyu!"

3. Je son de la feuli que l'aime

I love little Christ in the manger.
The horses watch o'er while He sleeps.
Mother Mary keeps Him from danger
As He's cuddled and warmed by sheep.
O, He is the Lamb of God,
Come here to save all mankind.
What miracle it is to see
This Jesus so gentle and kind!
Nativity! Nativity! Nativity!

4. Siempre los mascara

Shepherds watched o'er their sheep
In their dark night of the soul.
When suddenly, a dazzling light appeared
The shepherds their fear could not control.
But an angel spoke from the radiance,
Saying, "Shepherds, get thee away
To Bethlehem, where thou shalt see
The King of Kings this day."

5. Procession of the Three Kings (orchestra alone)

6. Ob vix abdurat (reprise)

7. Bozhe za kranit vsye

Weep no more, fear not, O man!
The Savior has come from th'Almighty's right hand
To banish woe here below
Although he bears the Cross' brand.

> Holy holy holy, heaven and earth are full of Thy glory.
> Praise ye!

8. Nemám dobrá se stále znova

The Christmas bells are chiming gaily,
Ringing out their gladsome strain
While men of cheer proclaim that Christ
Will cast out Satan's stain.
Sing the hymns with joy undimmed
And proudly hail the holy birth.
Rejoice that through our Lord and Savior
God is here on earth!

9. O die zimmer dank

O, this little child,
So innocent, meek, and mild,
Was borne here on angels' wings.
See how he smiles and how beguiles
All gathered round this holy ground,
Damp and cold, hours old. But behold
His face filled with heav'nly joy; this little boy
Gives charity and clarity to life.
Should others e'en feel my joy by half,
From delight they'd surely laugh.
Yes, yes! They would surely laugh!
Ha ha ha ha! They would surely laugh.
Should another feel my joy by half,
Then surely he would laugh.

10. Ob vix abdurat (reprise)

11. Spera dolci

Sweet hope, Redeemer, Savior,
These shalt Thou be when Thy day does come.
Rest for now, little baby Jesus,
Safe in your mother's arms,
Protected from all harm,
Angels will keep you warm.
This day is done.

* *

Although these "perductions" scan properly with the music to which they refer, these do not constitute translations *per se* of the actual *Karolju* foreign language texts. Rather, each serves as a precis of the expressive intent inherent in the music of each carol, and as such they should be printed, if desired, in the program book for listeners at concert performances of the entire score and be labeled as perductions. Under no circumstances should any part of *Karolju* be sung to these perducted texts, although it should be noted that full English texts do exist for liturgical performance of several appropriate carols from *Karolju*.

Further, it is essential that the foreign-language carol titles listed at the head of each perduction be listed only on the program page itself of the program book and not with the perductions, which presumably will follow or accompany actual program notes relating to the piece. On the program page, these titles should be listed vertically as follows:

Karolju (1990) *   Christopher Rouse (b. 1949)

    1. Ob vix abdurat
    2. Än kännas i på
    3. Je son de la feuli que l'aime
    4. Siempre los mascara
    5. Procession of the Three Kings (orchestra alone)
    6. Ob vix abdurat (reprise)
    7. Bozhe za kranit vsye
    8. Nemám dobrá se stále znova
    9. O die zimmer dank
    10. Ob vix abdurat (reprise)
    11. Spera dolci

* The date of composition for Karolju may be listed at the discretion of the performing organization.

C.R.

Christopher ROUSE

ORCHESTRA
Bump (1985)
Cello Concerto (1993)
Concerto Per Corde for String Orchestra (1990)
Contrabass Concerto (1985)
Gorgon (1984)
The Infernal Machine (1981)
Iscariot for Chamber Orchestra (1989)
Jagannath (1987)
Karolju for Chorus and Orchestra (1990)
Phaethon (1986)
Phantasmata (1981/85)
Symphony No. 1 (1986)
Trombone Concerto (1991)
Violin Concerto (1992)

ENSEMBLES
Artemis for Brass Quintet (1988)
Bonham for Eight Percussionists (1988)
Ku-Ka-Ilimoku for Four Percussionists (1978)
Lares Hercii for Violin and Harpsichord (1983)
Mitternachtlieder for Baritone and Ensemble (1979)
Ogoun Badagris for Five Percussionists (1976)
Rotae Passionis for Chamber Ensemble (1982)
String Quartet No. 1 (1982)
String Quartet No. 2 (1988)
The Surma Ritornelli for Chamber Ensemble (1983)

SOLOS
Liber Daemonum for Large Organ (1980)
Little Gorgon for Piano (1986)
Trarames for Carillon (1983)

HENDON MUSIC

BOOSEY & HAWKES

DISTRIBUTED BY
HAL•LEONARD CORPORATION
7777 W. BLUEMOUND RD. P.O. BOX 13819 MILWAUKEE, WI 53213